Fun with Cloth

By Cameron Macintosh

We can do lots of fun things with cloth.

Cloth can be thick.

It can be thin, too.

This cloth bag has a moth.

We can cut cloth.

When cloth rips,
we can fix it.

We can go to shops
to get cloth.

This shop has some
red cloth.

It can be pants or a hat!

We can put on cloth hats
to go in the sun.

Mish has a cloth hat
for when it's hot.

Seth is not hot.

Seth pops on a long cloth top to kick his ball.

Beth has a cloth doll.

It's a cloth sloth!

She can hang it up.

Nick has a dish cloth.

He rubs a wet dish with it.

Ming can put up a cloth tent!

She can sit in it all day with some snacks.

We can have lots of fun with cloth!

CHECKING FOR MEANING

1. Is cloth thick or thin? *(Literal)*

2. What things can we do with cloth? *(Literal)*

3. What else can Ming do in her cloth tent? *(Inferential)*

EXTENDING VOCABULARY

cloth	What are other words that have a similar meaning to *cloth*? E.g. fabric, material.
thick	Which word in the text is the opposite of *thick*?
dish	What are the three sounds in the word *dish*? Can you change the first sound to make new words?

MOVING BEYOND THE TEXT

1. What things do you have that are made of cloth?

2. Have you ever bought cloth at a shop? What did you need it for? What did you make from the cloth?

3. Talk about a time when you have had a rip in your clothes. What happened? How was it fixed?

4. What is a sloth? Where do they live? What do they eat? Find out some facts about sloths.

SPEED SOUNDS

| sh | ch | th | th | ck | ng |

voiced   unvoiced

PRACTICE WORDS

cloth

thick

moth

Mish

Cloth

Seth

long

kick

Beth

Nick

sloth

hang

things

Ming

dish

with

snacks